(www.E-Mediatebooks.com).

First edition: October 2020

ISBN: 978-0-9569989-6-5

Published by E-Mediate Books Ltd (www.E-Mediatebooks.com).

Working with...

SERVANT-LEADERSHIP

by

Charlie Foote

About Charlie Foote:

Charlie has been interested in Servant-Leadership since he first discovered it late in the 20th century. He was quickly introduced to The Greenleaf Centre for Servant-Leadership UK which held its first conference on Servant-Leadership in 1999. Charlie was there and has attended most of their annual conferences since then, and has presented at several. He has been a board member of the Centre for many years.

In 2013 Charlie also introduced an annual northern Servant-Leadership conference in Leeds. He has organised and presented at that conference.

As well as having theoretical knowledge, Charlie has introduced the principles of Servant-Leadership into several organisations, including three business he founded.

Sometimes the principles did not become permanent and the initiative has ended in failure. However, there was always a good reason, and Charlie took away valuable lessons. One thing that became clear to him is that a strong philosophical background was needed to bolster attempts to introduce Servant-Leadership.

Charlie tended to flounder when the going got tough – when, for example, senior colleagues became more interested in their own personal motives rather than the guiding motives of the organisation. He intends this book to go some way towards remedying a shortage of clearly stated, practical principles.

In 2006 Charlie founded Work AnyWare Ltd with Justin Gallagher. Work AnyWare was built from the start on Servant-Leadership principles, guided by Charlie's hard earned experience. It still runs as a Servant-Leadership organisation, and that influence is acknowledged on their web site. As a very successful business it shows that a Servant-Leadership based organisation can compete very effectively in a market economy.

CONTENTS

1 INTRODUCTION to SERVANT-LEADERSHIP

Servant-Leadership is a method of building and running organisations.

Its primary focus is on service. Hence the name Servant-Leadership. Leaders are seen as a servants of the organisation, of the organisation's purpose and of its people.

The leadership cares for its people and serves them in their best interests. However, it's not just me caring for you, or you caring for them, it's all of us caring for each other in a mutually supportive environment.

Sometimes we take a lead and sometimes not. We all work together so that no opportunity is missed and no activities are neglected in the service of our purpose – which is to serve our client base.

Imagine, if rail companies actually cared about travellers or online retailers really cared about their warehouse staff, it would be a better world for all of us.

If this sounds cuddly or soft-centred I can assure you it isn't. It's very difficult to do well, but well worth the effort!

Those organisations that use Servant-Leadership find that they are productive and profitable – they survive and thrive.

INTRODUCTION to the BOOK

This book is written to help you to understand Servant-Leadership and to give you some pointers if you want to give it a try.

It is an attempt to show the overall picture in one place – in a book which can be read quickly. It explains a coherent and consistent set of principles. It is a sort of overview which allows you to assess whether you want to use any, or all, of the techniques of Servant-Leadership.

Although the concept has been around for 50 years or so, it has found it hard to make ground in the finance-centred, free-market atmosphere of the last few decades.

There are clear signs that this is now changing.

Perhaps it is time for Servant-Leadership to come into its own.

I hope the book helps you to understand Servant-Leadership as something you can actually do. I hope it encourages you to try it in your organisation. I hope it supports you in your worthwhile efforts.

THEORY

Jan Taylor

"Can you give us a bit more detail about the box in the middle?"

2   THEORY

PHILOSOPHY

Servant-Leadership is a set of views and beliefs built on the original inspiration of Robert Greenleaf in 1970, the year he published his pamphlet *The Servant as Leader*.

To many of us Servant-Leadership is a philosophy – a way of thinking which we can apply to all aspects of life in organisations.

Much has been written about Servant-Leadership. It is a broad, rich and deep topic. A full treatment would require a much longer book than this one.

However, we can make lots of sample statements which, together, suggest a consistent idea and give life to the concept of Servant-Leadership.

The point of a philosophy of organisational behaviour is to turn it into practice. It can be done in many ways. This book is my personal way of doing it – and I hope it is in the true spirit of Servant-Leadership.

RESPECT

Servant-Leadership starts with true respect for our fellow human beings. If we truly understand respect for other human beings

–   recognising them

- having regard for their feelings
- caring for them
- preserving their dignity
- understanding their potential

then we already understand the basics of Servant-Leadership.

We build into our organisations respect for everyone. We get excellent results while feeling satisfied and fulfilled.

SERVICE

Servant-Leaders are exhorted to serve others in their best interests.

Some people don't like the words "servant" and "service". They think they have a demeaning connotation.

We can by all means call it something else: support, mutual support, care or even love.

But we serve – whatever we call it.

We find service a noble thing. We respect the task of service while respecting the people we serve, which we try to do willingly, tirelessly and helpfully.

And without any trace of servility.

LEADERSHIP

There are so many styles of leadership; dictatorial, transformational, military, charismatic, sporting, and so on. Servant-Leadership is one particular style of leadership, built on serving the needs of others in their best interests.

Too much has already been written about leadership in general to add much more here.

I'd just like to say that, in my view, all real leadership needs at least these factors:

- bringing the team together
- inspiring the team – providing the creative or imaginative spark
- triggering activities and events
- building and protecting the culture and values
- maintaining high standards

They are basic and indispensable components of leadership, whatever else we add to the mix.

Servant-Leaders don't fit the stereotype of "the great leaders" with an authoritative tone and an air of confidence and decisiveness.

They are more considered, considerate, collaborative and generally softer, and lead by inspiration and trust. It works for the organisation.

SERVANT-LEADERSHIP

Servant-Leadership is a seamless combination of service and leadership.

The Servant-Leader offers service first and then aspires to lead.

In our organisations we all aspire to be Servant-Leaders:

- sometimes leading
- sometimes helping others who lead
- always supporting others
- sometimes taking a leading initiative

Servant-Leadership creates a constructive environment where all can work in cooperation and collaboration, and builds a great community focusing on relationships between us.

Servant-Leadership operates best without a power hierarchy.

A spirit of service helps to lower a hierarchy – if I'm serving you I'm not setting myself above you.

BASICS

THE TENETS of SERVANT-LEADERSHIP

Servant-Leadership was proposed by Robert Greenleaf as a better means of running organisations. Here is my view of the basics which have emerged from the inspiration of Robert Greenleaf.

Many of these basics are, of course, relevant to any organisation, but Servant-Leadership offers them as a consistent set.

Servant-Leadership Organisations (SLOs)

SLOs must SURVIVE if they are to give service, and THRIVE so they can give the best service to the greatest number of recipients.

SLOs have a clear PURPOSE, or big idea, which is of primary importance and guides all their actions.

SLOs have a clear set of VALUES which guide their actions and are understood by everyone in the organisation.

SLOs exist to provide good products and service to as many people as possible for as long as possible – they do so with an attitude of STEWARDSHIP, working for the long run, with leaders acting as a stewards of the organisation.

SLOs meet the current and future needs of their CLIENT BASE, to the best of their ability – this is not only a philosophical imperative, but also helps the organisation to thrive.

SLOs are honourable and act with INTEGRITY

SLO's work in TEAMS which are mutually supportive and have a high level of autonomy – in an organisational structure which makes teamwork possible and effective.

SLO's first duty is to its EMPLOYEES – to offer worthwhile jobs and a chance to build successful careers in a supportive environment.

SLOs encourage and expect all employees to have an attitude of OWNERSHIP of the organisation – they are encouraged to participate in the running of the organisation leading, ultimately (and where relevant) to having a stake in the organisation.

SLOs ADVOCATE and promote Servant-Leadership, and create more Servant-Leaders, rather than followers.

Servant-Leaders (S-Ls)

S-Ls LEAD, not just manage.

S-Ls lead from the standpoint of SERVICE in the best interests of those served.

S-Ls SHARE POWER with those they work with and share decision making and the information needed to make sound decisions.

S-Ls act with COURAGE – feeling free do what is right – taking beneficial initiatives and resisting harmful interventions.

S-Ls show OPENNESS – listening to and accepting new ideas for enhancing service to the organisation's people and client base from whatever source they arise.

Colleagues

All the people in an SLO, including directors, operate from a mindset of unconditional mutual SUPPORT and full, unstinting collaboration and cooperation with their colleagues.

All the people in an SLO make a real CONTRIBUTION to the success of an SLO, being responsible, taking on responsibility, doing what needs doing, and developing as Servant-Leaders – and the organisation supports this.

OTHER BASICS

COOPERATION

Cooperation gives the best results.

Servant-Leadership organisations are built on cooperation – it's in our DNA – and we actively promote it.

Cooperating teams are a joy to work in. By working productively together morale improves, mutual trust grows, reciprocity is enhanced and the working environment becomes more enjoyable.

And by cooperation we get the best outcomes towards our common purpose – innovative, efficient and effective.

Our people and the organisation both really benefit.

We want everyone to cooperate and collaborate, internally and externally.

VIRTUOUS CIRCLE

A virtuous circle is a complex chains of events that reinforces itself through feedback, generating increasingly favourable results over time. (By the same token a vicious circle develops detrimental results).

In many ways Servant-Leadership is radical kindness. Something which Servant-Leaders feel comfortable with.

We are all people of emotion. If we are treated badly the resentment in us is visible to others and we may treat them badly. This spreads a feeling of unease. We are more likely to pass on that bad feeling to others we interact with.

But the opposite works. Kind behaviour spreads. It spreads far beyond your organisation. It affects families directly, and the wider community indirectly. It is a virtuous circle.

THE COMMON GOOD

> *"The benefits or interests of all,*
> *achieved by collective action"*

We care about the common good. It's not our prime motivation, but is there in our spectrum of concerns.

We always try to aid the common good unless it gets in the way of more immediate aims, such as support of our colleagues.

THE WIDER COMMUNITY

Servant-Leadership organisations keep the wider community in mind. We encourage our colleagues to support the local community, and we often offer sponsorship and direct financial support. For example by:

- sponsoring a local youth team
- hosting a street party
- giving financial support to families who foster or adopt
- donating to charity
- volunteering at a code club
- and many more

I'm not sure that this is a key part of Servant-Leadership but it is noticeable that organisations who practice Servant-Leadership often support the wider community in these sorts of ways.

DECISIONS

A lot of thought goes into making good decisions – it always takes effort.

In a non-emergency situation we can think in real time. We can afford the time and effort needed to reach the best decision.

In an emergency situation there is no time for this – we need quick decisive action. Hence we have to do the thinking before an emergency arises

Servant-Leadership, on a day-to-day basis, is concerned with the non-emergency situation. We listen to all opinions, seek evidence, discuss opinions and try to reach consensus. Which takes effort, and time, usually in a group environment.

In an emergency, decisions need to be made quickly and are based on rules of thumb backed up by experience of similar situations. Our detailed thinking has to be done before the emergency arises, developing sensible procedures and rehearsing them so, when the emergence happens we are ready.

In a state of emergency good leaders need to be confident and decisive.

Outside a state of emergency the Servant-Leadership approach results in the most efficient and effective decisions.

ORGANISATION

"You know what – this could be the
perfect symbol for all future organisations."
"But isn't the seat at the top
a bit precarious?"

Jan Taylor

3   THE ORGANISATION

VALUES

Servant-Leadership organisations are values-based.

We have a clear set of values and we write them down and live by them.

We favour organisational values such as:

- service
- integrity
- caring

But there is no "recommended set" for servant-leadership.

That's up to each organisation.

Here is an actual set of values taken from the web site of Work AnyWare Ltd, a Servant-Leadership Organisation:

Fairness In All That We Do

Respect In All Of Our Actions

Innovation In All That We Create

Commitment To All People

Humility In All Of Our Relationships

CULTURE

Culture is the sort of "internal atmosphere" of an organisation. It's the "way we do things here".

It's an expression of our values.

Culture arises in every organisation whether you plan it or not. It tends to arise from the way influential people do things – or disapprove of things.

So we need to provide a good example!

But culture can be worked on – and it is better for it.

Let's hold a full team meeting to discuss culture - "What should be part of it?" If the whole team works on it together we get a good culture which everyone understands. New people easily fit into it.

In a great culture it easy to do your best.

SERVANT-LEADERSHIP CULTURE

Here are some ideas which fit in well with a Servant-Leadership culture.

- cooperation at all times
- mutual respect
- enthusiasm valued
- personal initiative valued
- no blame – avoiding a climate of fear
- each has their say
- serious purpose but fun achieving it
- celebrating success
- work life balance
- diversity

NO BLAME

A no-blame culture is not exclusive to Servant-Leadership, but fits well with it.

There are two sorts of no-blame culture:

1)   A culture when we admit our mistakes and near misses so that we can all learn from them – this is often used in areas where safety is vital, such as with pilots and surgeons

2)   A culture where we can take the risk of trying new things – with no adverse effects on us if they don't work out – this is often used in the IT and creative industries where the mantra might be "Celebrate mistakes" – if we aren't making mistakes we aren't being brave enough.

Both sorts are encouraged in a Servant-Leadership organisation.

We don't fear mistakes. It's what comes next that's important. If we reach for something new and don't quite make it, we can modify and try again.

We have in our minds an image of what we want to achieve. A mis-step doesn't change that image. In an Servant-Leadership environment we see a mis-step as a learning exercise.

EMOTIONS

There is plenty of scientific evidence that we humans need emotional thinking as well as rational thinking.

The values of our Servant-Leadership organisations are reflections of our emotional rather than rational thinking. And our purpose is founded in emotional thinking.

Emotions provide drive and determination and inform many of our supposedly rational judgements. To really get behind a purpose it needs to be linked in some way with our emotions.

Rational thinking, on the other hand, ensures that our emotions don't go wild, and that we carefully consider our ways forward, and make sensible plans and strategies to achieve our purpose.

Servant-Leadership with its stress on serving people in their best interests has a clear emotional thinking component.

Servant-Leadership also promotes using all the brains in the organisation through sharing power and making shared decisions in teams.

SIGNALS

All organisations need to effectively react to their environment:

- to sense incoming signals
- to quickly check if they mean danger
- to evaluate and review the messages we are receiving
- to take action in response
- to ensure that any action doesn't compromise other actions we may be taking

We receive signals from internal and external sources.

Internal signals are messages or hints about the way the organisation is operating.

Are the people reasonably content?
Are people under too much stress?
Are people adequately trained for facing the future?
Are our internal processes working effectively?

External signals are message or hints about changes in the environment in which the organisation is operating.

Is our client base reasonably content?

Are competitors moving into our market space?

Are regulations changing which affect us?

Is accepted technology changing?

Both sorts have to be processed.

SIGNAL PROCESSING

Common signals are figures and numbers which are clear signals, and we occasionally carry out planned surveys to get feedback. But there is another sort of signal which is often missed: those which are picked up by our people in the course of their daily activities.

In a Servant-Leadership organisation our people are our sensors. We encourage everyone to act as if they were owners of the organisation – hence they are on the lookout for the beginnings of problems, and keen to share their findings.

It is too often the case that the signals are clearly there, but no one is listening. We ensure every person is aware and our no blame culture means they are not afraid to raise negative or worrying issues. No comment is too insignificant.

The team meeting is a place where all internal signals are put on the table and assessed, and if action is needed it is added to the appropriate plan.

SUCCESS

Success is independent of philosophy.

People with a wonderfully caring and respectful philosophy can succeed – or can fail. People with a rapacious and greedy philosophy can succeed – or can fail.

For Servant-Leaders success means:

- surviving now and into the future
- growing enough to:
  - keep up with the market
  - give real opportunities to our people
  - building an effective and happy community within the organisation where people
    - grow as people and develop their skills
    - feel they are contributing to something bigger
    - get real satisfaction and meaning from their work
    - cooperate with each other

thus making a contribution to the wider world.

STEWARDSHIP

We build our organisations to last.

We see ourselves as taking care of the organisation so that we can pass on to the next generation, when the time comes, in good order.

The Servant-Leadership attitude to organisations is that they are there for ever.

The leaders see themselves as being stewards of a permanent organisation.

We are all fallible and many individual leaders think of selling their organisation to reap personal financial rewards.

For that reason many Servant-Leadership organisations build in a mechanism to endure it cannot be sold or merged with others for personal profit. For example, by issuing one or more golden shares.

POWER and AUTHORITY

True Servant-Leaders share their power with teams.

Leaders may be brilliant and competent and dynamic and forward looking. While they may understand their own value, they don't inflate it – Servant-Leaders don't go lusting after power and the trappings of power for their own sake.

Servant-Leaders have natural authority from leading from a standpoint of service.

We can share power by putting decision before the team for discussion and decision.

We maintain a low power distance, and hesitate to share power with those people who are keenest to get power – they tend to use it badly.

ACCOUNTABILITY

The terms "accountability" and "responsibility" are often used interchangeably.

For the purposes of this book we use accountability to mean the one who carries the can, and responsibility as the one who does the work. They may, of course, both be invested in the same person.

We believe accountability can be shared, just as leadership and power can be shared.

Servant-Leadership teams want to feel accountable as well as responsible. They often voluntarily take on accountability and share it with each other and with other teams in the organisation.

Team members can contribute to shared accountability by holding each other to account – in a supportive way.

STRUCTURE

Organisations need some sort of structure to be effective. It can be minimal – such as "the founder and everyone else". But mostly we need something a little more than that.

Servant-Leadership organisations minimise power structures, although in practice most Servant-Leadership organisations have them to some extent.

We aim for as low a hierarchy as possible and any structure should support team working.

There are alternatives to hierarchies. One such is circular organisation, in which each circle is a group whose members have equal status. There will usually be a spokesperson who may represent the circle to other circles. That person may be called a "first among equals".

It is usually necessary for units (or circles) within an organisation to coordinate with each other for the good of the organisation. For example, the manufacturing circle needs some idea of the sales which the sales circle might be achieved.

The circles overlap, with one or more members being a member of both circles to allow effective coordination.

HIERARCHY

Steep hierarchies of power are old fashioned – most large commercial organisations are trying to lower them.

However, hierarchies are ubiquitous. They are rarely questioned because they are ingrained in our psyches as the way to run things.

In Servant-Leadership we aim for a low hierarchy or no hierarchy at all.

Hierarchies arose historically because workers didn't know what to do, or were reluctant to do it – or both.

Workers were often uneducated, maybe not even literate, so being clearly instructed, at a detailed level, was important. Jobs could be dull, dirty or dangerous. Without a hierarchy of power the workers wouldn't do the jobs at all.

Some people argue that we need hierarchies so that we have opportunities to promote our people in recognition of their hard work and good results.

There is something in this. We have to try to find alternative ways of recognition so as not to build a steep hierarchy.

TEAMS

"Thought so – a few loose egos – that's your problem."

4   TEAMS

TEAMS

Servant-Leadership is very keen on team working. Why?

For the organisation, teams:

- are effective – give excellent results
- utilise all the brains in the organisation to get the best decisions
- produce ideas which a lone thinker might not arrive at, hence increase innovation
- help to form a flatter structure, with less hierarchy
- encourage flexibility, responsiveness and creativity
- encourage a sense of ownership of the work

For the team members, they:

- like working in teams
- have a sense of mutual support and belonging
- have a feeling of accomplishment when things go well
- have a social impact – we are social beings
- feel a sense of equality and fairness
- are motivated to do their best work

We typically use teams with fewer than 10 members; six is a good size.

Team members have equal status within the team, although some members may be more experienced.

There will usually be a team spokesperson. Sometimes called a team leader, and sometimes a "first among equals".

SELF-ORGANISING

Self-organising teams can be highly effective. They take on their purpose and objectives and understand the resources available to them. They, themselves, decide how they are going to use the resources to achieve their purpose.

Self-organising teams work well in Servant-Leadership organisation because:

- they use the knowledge of the people actually doing the work to decide how the work should be done – and are trusted to do it

- they are aware of the needs of their clients and customers because they are frequently interacting with them, and have the authority to take steps which they know are needed (without waiting for bureaucratic confirmation)

- they are motivated by the great sense of autonomy which self-organising gives them

- they feel accountable and responsible for all they do

We try to make all our teams as self-organising as possible.

TEAM MEETINGS

Our team meetings aim to be:

- regular
- structured
- friendly but efficient
- without display of rank
- attended by everyone – no excuses

We use a standard agenda with places for (at least)

- announcements
- items for discussion
- items for decision

We encourage any employee to raise any item in any of these categories.

All topics get fully and fairly aired.

If decisions are required we make them by consensus or consent.

TEAM DECISIONS

We make decisions in teams. Team decision making has pros and cons, but we make sure we build on the pros and minimise the cons.

THE PROS

Teams use all the available brainpower to get the best, most creative ideas.

Teams utilise a variety of viewpoints to come up with ideas outside any one person's creativity horizon.

Teams come up with lots of ideas.

Teams evaluate those ideas more effectively – they receive the most thorough scrutiny and analysis.

The effort the team puts into making the right decision means that we get the best support and buy-in from the team members.

CONDITION

These benefits only accrue if the team consists of independent minds, in an atmosphere where suggestions are accepted (and never put down) and the team members are carefully listened to by the group.

THE CONS

Group decision making takes time.

There are a few dangers which the protocol has to account for and overcome. The main ones are:

- "groupthink"
- "political parties"
- "free loading"

"Groupthink" is where the group thinks it has to agree with the group leader and supports that view without much personal thought. A mild version of this is where the view of the first person to speak influences he rest of the conversation.*

"Political parties" is where a subgroup gets together and argues as a bloc. They might even give themselves a name such as ("We are the growth group").

"Free loading" is where group members come to a meeting with no intention of contributing.

A simple tip with a contentious issue is to get everybody to write down their opinion before discussion starts, and show their written statement when it's their turn to speak. Otherwise the first person to speak may have undue influence. And we get the most influential person to speak last not first.

DECISION PROTOCOL

A typical Servant-Leadership decision protocol would include

- regular meetings
- fixed agendas
- anyone can raise an item for discussion or decision
- all items given a fair hearing – everyone speaks
- no blame culture
- no voting – it only creates unhappy people
- use consensus or at least willing consent

After fully, and carefully, discussing all the discussion, the chair (which we circulate) proposes what she or he thinks is the shared view of the meeting. If everyone assents, consensus is reached and the decision is made

If some people dissent, we keep talking. If no consensus appears, we ask the dissenter if she or he will fully support the decision. If yes, consent is reached and the decision is made If at least one person can't consent then there are options

- We revert to the status quo
- We reframe the question and start again
- We put in place some mitigations which can help the dissenter consent to the decision

FREEDOM of INFORMATION

Great teams make great decisions – but only if they have the information they need. We make sure the teams have all this information.

No information is secret – we share it all. We present it to them – maybe on wall charts or screens – we don't make them ask, however willing we are to share it.

We don't make them come for it, because they won't.

Perhaps they don't want to disturb us.

TARGETS

Particularly in the public sector targets are often imposed externally in an attempt to increase the achievement of measurable outcomes.

While there is a place for targets, they do have side effects.

- They affect things not aimed at, such as morale

- They encourage people to meet the targets at the expense of more worthy aims

- Especially when combined with financial incentives, they motivate people to game the system

- They can generate internal competition which can waste time and effort.

Eventually targets become less effective and even stop working.

Servant-Leadership discourages the use of targets imposed from the outside. If a team wants to put targets on its own performance that's healthy or they may happily accept a generalised target for the good of the organisation, eg "please bring in 50 sales".

We don't set targets which encourage competition between our people who may try to achieve them at the expense of others.

PEOPLE

"A human being answered the phone!"

5 PEOPLE

INTRODUCTION

Servant-Leadership is about people. Nothing is done without people.

We treat people well and they respond by treating each other well and treating our client base well.

We need the best people we can get – those with the most potential and the right attitudes. Once on board we give everyone a chance to grow and to develop, and encourage them to take it.

Sometimes people grow into unexpected roles.

The people we serve are in four broad groups, and we try to serve them in all we do. However, if there is a clash of interests, we serve them in this order:

- **Our people**
- **Served people**
- **Local people**
- **All people**

Our people are our colleagues.

Served people are those which our organisation serves

If a shop   - customers

If a hospital   - patients
If a lawyer   - clients
If a ship   - passengers
If a benefits office   - people with financial hardship*

Taken together we call them our "client base".
Local people are those in the local communities in which our organisation is embedded.

All people is wider society and the common good where we can be a beacon of goodwill and good sense.

*   *I'm not sure that benefit offices see themselves as "serving" claimants - but they are called "civil servants".*

HOW WE TREAT PEOPLE

We treat people well, respecting diversity and we encourage them and help them to grow and develop.

As Servant-Leaders our desire is to serve our colleagues in their best interests.

We help colleagues to feel secure and grounded since this is a launchpad from which they will fly – giving us their best efforts.

We confirm in our colleagues a clear sense of purpose.

We provide a working atmosphere in which they can motivate themselves to do their best work and we help them improve their skills

We help them to get better. We encourage them to grow as people and to take on more responsibility when the time is right.

UNCONDITIONAL SUPPORT

We want everyone in our organisation to have a mindset of unconditional support. In a community of supportive colleagues everyone can do their best work.

Unconditional support is a mindset – it's a basic motivation for what we do. We call it a mindset rather than an imperative because we accept that we can't always support people the way they would want, but we can always try our best to do so.

We can do our best to support the person, in all circumstances, although we may not be able to support their behaviour in any particular instance.

If all colleagues support each other, in their mutual best interests, we generate an ideal workplace – efficient, effective, meaningful and enjoyable.

EQUALITY and FAIRNESS

Individuals are different. They are born with different levels of intelligence, empathy, ball sense, social skill etc. and their lives take on different trajectories.

However, everyone is a fellow human being and deserves to be dealt with equal care and respect.

To Servant-Leadership "equal" relates to equality of impact, rather than equality of treatment.

Suppose, in a downturn, you have to ask the staff to take a small pay cut. One person lives at home with his parents, and another is the father of a disabled child, whose mum can't take paid work because of caring for the child.

The impact of a pay cut will be very different on each.

In my experience my colleagues would not wish equal treatment on these two people – they would respect that the impact on the second person is too high. They would rather take a slightly larger cut themselves than see that person's life disrupted.
And, of course, the leadership should take the largest cut of all.

Our sense of fairness is the process of taking everyone seriously, and do our best for them, bearing in mind their different circumstances.

A strict 9 am start may make a single mum always late, and a bad employee.

Changing her start time to 9.15 am may make her the most consistently on time and a great employee.

SENSE of COMMUNITY

We make our workplace a community and actively build a community feel.

People like to feel part of a community – we have a human instinct to care for and support each other.

We make sure everyone is brought into the community at work.

People who are grounded in a community, who feel secure and supported, are ready to fly. They will give us superb work and dedication.

We often feel that the modern workplace tends to remove a sense of community – in Servant-Leadership we really want to get it back.

ENJOYMENT

An important point about an Servant-Leadership working environment is that it's enjoyable while being productive. Fun is important. There are challenges to enjoy, progress to feel good about and achievements to celebrate.

We look forward to coming to work. We enjoy being a part of a community at work – caring for others and being cared for. We enjoy socialising with the people we work with.

Unhappiness doesn't make you more efficient, effective or productive. Think about this in relation to yourself – does it?

MOTIVATION

We can't motivate people directly, but we can create an atmosphere in which they will motivate themselves and surprise us with the quality of their creativity and effort.

People are widely thought to be motivated by purpose, autonomy and mastery. They want to know what they are doing, have some say in how they do it and can get better at it.

A Servant-Leadership organisation has a clear purpose.

A Servant-Leadership organisation is built from teams with autonomy, so that the people actually doing the work have a clear say in how it's done.

A Servant-Leadership organisation supports learning of all sorts, including internal learning such as mentoring and external training. For example, we may have a training budget which the employee can spend on any course they like – with no strings attached.

WHAT WE LOOK FOR

We look for people who "get" Servant-Leadership, who have the potential to do good work and who will fit in with our culture.

We look for people who can work with others with mutual respect, cooperation and honest feedback, who bring their full self to work, and who can work effectively for the purpose of the organisation. In particular we look for people who:

- have the ability to work in teams
- have the ability to cooperate
- feel good about supporting and be supported
- have a low hierarchy mindset
- are prepared to be creative and contribute to ideas sessions
- are able and have potential
- have a mature view of work
- are trusting and trustworthy
- have respect for the humanity of all colleagues

BEHAVIOURS

Behaviour is what we do. Most behaviours are of no concern to the organisation. But some are.

We specifically state broad outlines of expected behaviour and make them clear at the recruitment stage. If people don't want to behave that way they don't have to join the organisation.

We use our general standard of behaviour in recruitment, induction, general day-to-day involvement and appraisal.

We particularly discourage internal competition. Within an organisation competition and competitiveness are corrosive. They destroy the cooperation which is so essential to our success.

We encourage cooperation between teams and between individuals. Cooperation brings the best results and joy for all. In a low hierarchy we all need good interpersonal skills. There is no external authority to regulate behaviour. We use adult-to-adult conversations, listening and attending respectfully to the views of others and stating our own clear opinions calmly.

RESPONSIBILITY

Our people take responsibility for what they are doing at work.

In our "no-blame" culture we value people who take responsibility and try to do better things, or do things in a better way.

If they don't quite make it we don't want them to feel blamed. If they are, they will be reluctant to take on responsibility in the future.

This doesn't mean anyone can do anything without a care for the consequences. All of us in the organisation must have in their mind, and feel responsible for, meeting the ultimate purpose of the organisation as effectively as we can.

FINDING the RIGHT PEOPLE

Getting the right people as colleagues in Servant-Leadership organisations is vitally important. We recruit for attitude not performance.

We recruit at the entry level – new graduates if appropriate – and watch them grow with our support.

We promote from within – hence we only employ people with potential – and the right attitude.

Cultural fit is vital.

Every organisation uses whatever practical procedure suits them. We recommend:

- Treating CVs with a large pinch of salt – they don't help much and are open to misrepresenting the candidate – I personally don't ask for them.

- Taking plenty of time – it's an important decision for you and the applicant.

- Meeting face-to-face for long enough.

- Involving many people, including the whole team they are likely to join.

- If any of those who meet the candidate expresses a reservation, we don't take on that candidate.

I have failed to do this on many occasions and got the wrong people who were disruptive and took up far too much time that should have been spent meeting our purpose.

JOB DESCRIPTIONS

We don't use written ones – or we keep them very simple. And they should be based on responsibilities rather than tasks.

The simplest I've heard is "Do cool stuff".

Written job descriptions can become straight jackets. They can tie down our creative people.

People want to do good work – we don't let job descriptions get in the way of this. We don't let conventional thinking bully us into doing what we think is unhelpful.

DISTRIBUTION of TASKS and JOBS

There are some sensible rules which we use to make delegation work. Such as:

- delegate objectives not tasks
- challenge the person taking on the task, but don't outface them.

But is delegation a good word to use in a Servant-Leadership organisation? It carries an implication of giving part of your work to somebody else. It has a ring of a power hierarchy about it.

Teams should be looking out for what needs doing and voluntarily taking it on. Of course in any complex organisation there needs to be coordination. We can do it in a non-hierarchical way with teams "taking on objectives" rather than "being given objectives".

The difference relates to motivation – we are more motivated to do what we take on that to do what we are told.

And we never delegate stress.

RECOGNITION

Our people work hard. Like all human beings they like their work to be recognised and rewarded.

In a low hierarchy recognition by promotion can be difficult because there are fewer slots to promote people into.

We might sometimes be able to promote people, even in a low hierarchy, but often we can't. So we have to find other means of recognition.

It's important to be creative about recognition.

We can try all sort of approaches, such as job titles, specialities, "first among equals", representing the firm externally, attendance at global conferences of whatever.

In a low hierarchy, with fewer available slots, it is very damaging to morale to bring in higher level people from outside. So we don't do it.

Servant-Leaders use their emotion feel to understand what motivates each individual, and to recognise and reward them accordingly.

We don't want to lose good people because they feel that they aren't being recognised.

MOVING PEOPLE ON

Some people don't fit into an Servant-Leadership culture. As long as we are recruiting human beings we are bound to occasionally get one that doesn't fit – that we missed when recruiting.

They may choose to move on themselves. If they don't we may have to help them to move on.

Some of those who don't fit can be persuaded to change – and we make every effort to help them and they can stay. Sadly most people are unable to change.

We must move on those who are immune to change.

A difficult person can be grit in the machine. A small thing that can jam the gears – and bring our efforts to a halt.

DIFFICULT PEOPLE

Step 1: We try to help them to stay. We show them we care. We help them to change. We send them on courses. We provide a mentor. We give them a fair chance to change.

Step 2: If they can't change we start the process of moving them on. We may be able to locate an opportunity for them elsewhere. – or possibly pay for retraining so they can get a good job elsewhere. If we care about their well being, and they are reasonable people, we will reach a solution.

Step 3: If they are intransigent and no solution is possible, then we firmly get rid of them. There will be a cost, but it's better to accept that than to risk having our culture and our effectiveness compromised. Our care for the organisation and all the people in it must overrule our care for a particular toxic individual. Hence we are determined – we don't give up – our organisation depends on it.

CLIENT BASE

"....and this is the figure for customer retention since we cut back on service."

6 CLIENT BASE

CLIENT BASE

Our client base is the people which it is our purpose to serve.

Our client base may consist of:

- – customers
- – clients
- – travellers
- – patients
- – unemployed people
- – children
- – animals (and their owners)
- – parishioners

Or whoever we serve.

THE OFFER

The offer is what we offer our client base.

We make it as good as possible. And surround it with trust and integrity.

We always treat people in the client base as human beings. They are not numbers or tickets.

We really listen to them and their suggestions and complaints. They will sense that we care, and from their feedback we will improve our product and service, with their help.

In the private sector we will have a happy client base and they will happily recommend us to others.

It is essential that we build in a mechanism that allows change as a result of feedback (see next section).

ASLEEP at the WHEEL

If we don't know what our client base is thinking we are asleep at the wheel – and heading for a crash.

Sometimes our front line staff are aware of the danger and shout their concerns, but we aren't listening. We are still asleep at the wheel, and still heading for a crash.

In far too many situations everyone is awake, but no one wants the responsibility of grabbing the wheel and changing course. Still heading for a crash.

A problem with the public, charitable and private sectors, if not led by Servant-Leaders, is that their vehicles can career on, not fully in control and no one taking the wheel. Be a Servant-Leader and grab that wheel!

BUILDING

Building the client base is part of sales and marketing. As such, Servant-Leadership doesn't have much to say which isn't covered in more detail elsewhere.

However, referrals are the best way to build the client base.

Servant-Leadership, with its focus on great service and support, tends to generate referrals.

We listen to and care for clients – never being misleading or dishonest with them.

We are creative in ways of building our client base. It helps that Servant-Leadership organisations are by nature creative.

SUPPORT and SERVICE

We give the best service and support we can.

- It feels right
- It's honourable
- It has a good effect on our organisation

We never see support and service as a cost – if we do someone will try to minimise it. And this will have a bad effect on our organisation's reputation

We have a mindset of unconditional support – too many firms (banks?) say this, but their behaviour belies their words.

STANDARDS

Setting and maintaining standards is a key responsibility of leadership.
Client support and service standards have a tendency to drift downwards. We are not quite sure why. Maybe new staff don't really understand our huge emphasis on client support.

As Servant-Leaders one of our most vital roles is to set a very high standard for support of our client base – our customers, our partners, our claimants and to ensure that this standard doesn't accidentally drift downwards over time.

That leadership also needs to ensure that support and service are seen as part of our genuine offer to the client base and not an expensive add-on.

HUMAN and IT

We always use human beings for human interactions.

We use humans where humans are best and IT where IT is best.

Artificial Intelligence can be helpful – but as an intelligent aid to humans, not a replacement for humans.

Let's not mix up the two.

People are seriously annoyed if they have to ring us and can't get through. How much do people with automated telephone systems care about their customers? The impression they give is that they don't.

MONEY

7   MONEY

PROFIT

We don't get hung up on profit.

Profit is like water to you and me. It's essential for survival, but no one drinks as much water as possible.

We must have enough profit – we cannot do without it. After that it's just a scorecard.

Excess profit steals from our employees and our customers.

If we are passionate about what we do we see the results in peoples' faces – we don't need to look at figures.

We free ourselves from the tyranny of profit.

GROWTH

Growth, like profit, is a scorecard.

As an organisation we should want:

- to survive and thrive
- to give people a chance to grow and to develop
- to have a sustainable and secure client base

- to have enough funds to invest in creative new ideas

Once we have these things we don't need to worry any more about further growth – it'll happen anyhow.

We don't aim to stop growth – we let it happen. It's natural if we are running a sound organisation.

PAY

We pay people well.

Creative people are most effective when money is not an issue in their daily lives – when they don't have to worry about money.

We don't use monetary rewards as incentives – they don't work (mostly) and can make things worse.

We offer interesting work and people surprise us with how well they contribute to the success of the organisation. They motivate themselves.

If we employ a targets and a bonus culture people start to game the system and even compete with their colleagues, to the detriment of real, useful work.

Bonuses are OK if given after the event – a reward not an incentive.

We might set the size of a bonus pot and let the employees decide how to divide it up.

We don't call pay "compensation" – that makes it sound that work is so horrible we have to compensate people for turning up.

RESERVES

Reserves sounds like the dullest subject ever... but ...

Reserves are just an emergency fund which can be used either:

- to keep us going when things go wrong

or

- to allow us to take on good initiatives when they arise.

In either case we have enhanced freedom and flexibility.

The freedom to keep going even in hard times and the flexibility to try new things and fund our aspirations.

Without reserves we may have to fall back on banks – at times of need they tend to have the upper hand.

We try to keep a good positive bank balance. We don't use overdraft funding if we can avoid it.

8   POSTSCRIPT

"Shall we use Servant-Leadership?"

POSSIBILITIES

Using Servant-Leadership opens up possibilities.

It is open-ended and generous.

Bureaucratic or command and control approaches close down possibilities. To these approaches an element of freedom can appear threatening to their control.

If we can let go of this fear of lack of control we will find that people who are offered supportive freedom become energetic, creative and effective. They don't become anarchic – we need to let go of the fear that they might.

The ideas of Robert Greenleaf can be said to undermine the authority of the conventional wisdom which says people need to be commanded and controlled and that a clear hierarchy is the "common sense" way of running an organisation.

It is a misapprehension to believe that we all have to be saints to run a Servant-Leadership organisation. It is a forgiving approach. We make mistakes – perhaps we don't support each other as we should, or we get angry and frustrated. However, we tolerate these excesses and learn from them, without harming the basic concept.

Organisational theory has for a number of years now considered softer, more people-centred organisations. The current zeitgeist is to move in that direction.

Robert Greenleaf gave a substantial impetus to this way of thinking.

MY EXPERIENCE

I have tried over my working career to introduce into my various workplaces the concepts of Servant-Leadership (since I discovered it in the 1970s).

I have tried it without much backup of theory or practice. And I have had many failures.

I failed to have Servant-Leadership accepted by other people in the organisations I worked in – although individual techniques I introduced have sometimes lived on.

I didn't then have a grasp of the techniques to use – or the confidence to really try them. I didn't know how the various techniques linked together, the philosophy, and I didn't have an answer when things didn't seem to work, or when naysayers complained that I should "get real".

As time went on I got better at it. I got more persuasive, and more able to defend my approach against those with a more conventional outlook.

VERDICT

To the question "Shall we use Servant-Leadership?" the short answer, of course, is "Yes".

Organisational behaviour covers a vast territory and there are a few useful maps. Servant-Leadership is one such map.

The map can lead us to our ultimate destination. It helps by giving us a language in which we can describe the organisation we want to be, and the way we want to get there.

If you have read this far you will be one of those people who "get it" – to whom Servant-Leadership seems obvious – and it will feel like the right thing to be doing.

We hope this book provides some useful waypoints on the route.

Lightning Source UK Ltd.
Milton Keynes UK
UKHW021032271220
375899UK00014B/1557

9 780956 998965